Damn!

a
C H R I S T M A S
book with sex
VIOLENCE
drugs &
FRUITCAKE

THE ABERRANT ART OF BARRY KITE

Pomegranate

San Francisco

Published by Pomegranate Communications, Inc.
Box 6099, Rohnert Park, CA 94927

Pomegranate Europe Ltd.
Fullbridge House, Fullbridge
Maldon, Essex CM9 4LE, England

All photocollages reproduced herein are made from 100% recycled images and contain no added drawing or painting or anything requiring more skill than cutting up old art books and magazines and pasting the pieces back together so that they finally become relevant to life as it exists on this planet today.—B.K.

For a catalog and information regarding the availability of individual greeting cards pictured in this book, call 1-800-99KITE1 or www.aberrantart.com.

ISBN 0-7649-0688-7
Pomegranate Catalog No. A503

Library of Congress Cataloging-in-Publication Data
Kite, Barry.
    Damn! : a Christmas book with sex, violence, drugs &
    fruitcake / the aberrant art of Barry Kite
            p.   cm.
        ISBN 0-7649-0688-7 (hc : alk. paper)
        1. Kite, Barry—Themes, motives. 2. collage, American.
    3. Christmas cards—United States. I. Title
    N6537.K54A4   1998
    709'.2—dc21   98-21509
                        CIP

Printed in China
07 06 05 04 03 02 01 00 99   10 9 8 7 6 5 4 3 2

First Edition

CONTENTS

The Introduction   4

The Art   7

The List of Plates   63

About the Artist   64

THE INTRODUCTION

When the Pope first asked me to design some Christmas cards, I was initially shocked. How the hell did he get my private number? Didn't he realize what time it was here? How would he like to be woken up at ten in the morning? Was it perhaps that the flood of Hallmarkian holiday greetings that had been circulating for generations had become tiring and outdated—aspartamic self-parodies? Who is this, really?

Since we're all well aware of the American addiction to self-fulfillment and soul-searching, it should not come as a surprise to anyone (except for a few people in small, isolated, rural communities without call forwarding) that we have pretty much stopped, as a people, writing personal notes of greeting to anyone. We choose our feelings instead from a catalog of pre-felt sentiments, beautifully inscribed on mass-produced "greeting cards." At no time of year is this national habit more apparent than that period of time encompassing November and December known as "The Holidays."

But what about those enduring, truer inner feelings that we bury deep inside ourselves? Those feelings that pointedly express who we are, where we come from, and where we would like to go, if only we had the time and the money? These feelings are often so personal and unique that the closest we ever come to communicating them to the people in our lives to whom they would matter the most is when we select an off-the-rack "Christmas card," with red foil bells and "boughs of holly" on the cover, and scratch out the printed

"Wishing You and Yours the Most Joyous . . ." on the inside and write in large and shaky script, often blurred by an errant teardrop, in red lipstick, the poignant plea: "HELP ME!" As if anyone would actually open and read such a card before standing it up on the mantel above the gas-powered, Presto-logged fireplace next to the other unfeeling visions of nativity scenes, sleigh rides, fat men in red suits, and, of course, personalized portraits of empty, unhappy families with those phony, sneering smiles that say, "Another year with these losers. How in the hell can I stand it?" And those babies in their red and green sweaters are the worst.

Where was I?

So, finally, taking matters into my own hands, I decided to establish a presence in the Holiday Greeting Card Market, or rather in the long-neglected niche in that market, which strives to satisfy people with big hearts who need a voice to tell those they care about that: "Hey, we think this Christmas card crap is just a big commercial hype that's been forced up our you-know-whats for too long, and we just want to give you a wink and a nod because we know that you, being an enlightened twenty-first-century thinker and all, agree; and that because we love you, and really care, and want world peace and everything, we're sending an anti-Christmas card because, well, because, well . . . you know."

But since the very nature of greeting cards is that you're supposed to buy them specifically to send to someone else, and that you would appear rather selfish and reclusive if you just bought them and kept them—because you really didn't want to just be stuck with the ones that other people sent you—I felt it was time to offer a collection of these images in book form. Then you wouldn't feel so embarrassed about keeping the images yourself. Better yet, we'll call it a gift book, so that when your in-laws come over and happen to find it, you can tell them it was a gift. And you don't talk to that person anymore.

Many of the images contained in this collection have been or are currently being published (under my Aberrant Art logo) as greeting cards. Some of the designs have not yet been printed and come straight from the design table (what a treat for you!). Five years ago, when I first began doing these cards, I solicited feedback from friends, retailers, and sales reps carrying my line of everyday notecards. For the most part the reaction was that Christmas was too sacred an institution to make fun of. People were just too sensitive to tolerate Santa Claus being shot, hanged, hit by an airplane, dropped from the sky, cryogenically preserved, or disemboweled. You couldn't have Rudolph being eaten alive or even sliced up, much less get him laid, have his nose fixed, or sell him to a butcher. You couldn't serve the Virgin Mary liquor; you definitely could not pickle elves. Snowmen were asexual and nonthreatening. No one mixed cadavers and fruitcake! I considered these objections.

For about this long.

I no longer underestimate the repressed angst of the American public.

And I'm here for you.   —Barry Kite

THE ART

Damn!

Hazards Incumbent in the Adaptation of Traditional Myth
to a Redefined Urban Ecosystem

Turbulence

Where have we come
from? How did we get here? Who were
our ancestors? These questions have
haunted humankind ever since he drew
his first breath... reached out for the heavens.
From Neanderthal to Cro Magnon to
Turkana Boy (OK, we've made up)
Turkana Boy and Peking Man (etc.)
not to mention anthropologists and
archeologists have been putting
together the pieces of the puzzle
that is the human race. Almost daily
new finds tell us more of our
evolution. The earth no longer
held that... and the only
remains of our... have led to
the... the only one that means
this and the... with
the half of one could only mean
that... Anyway, until we... will we
ever know the truth?

North Pole Man

Well, look at
that! It's Admiral Byrd. He has
finally made it to the North Pole,
as we can tell by Frederic Church's
Aurora Borealis in the background.
But wait. Someone's beat him to it.
Five snowmen are already there and
taking a group picture. Looks like
their Karmann Ghia took quite a
beating getting there.

   This image—at first appearing
packed with the fun and exuberance
of a vacation slide—I had always
wanted a Karmann Ghia, until
circumstances forced me to buy a
van—soon descends into the depth of
disillusion as the revered admiral
realizes his dreams of international
fame and respect are now crushed.
His cronies at the Explorer's Club
will deride his failure to be first
to the Pole by periodically dressing
up as snowmen and sitting in the
leather chairs next to him, puffing
their pipes and disparaging about
the cost of bodywork on their Ghia.

Expedition

...'s that special
time of year again, when all
institutions make the switch over
from their normal, everyday,
business-as-usual mentalities to
those festive humors that uplift
the spirit and call for increased
medication.

Here, however, an extra-special
dose of holiday "upliftium" is
called for. One of the group has
uniformly chosen to "default" to a
nonseasonal format (David's
Napoleon).

In this image, the infectious
"holiday spirit" is symbolized by a
pill. (Would that love and good
will were so easy to convey!)
Napoleon represents that strong
sense of individualism that resists
those quintessential pressures of society
who choose to remember Dave, the
floods of commercial and quasi-
religious sentiments. Also Jews,
Muslims, Buddhists, Hindus, and
people with little choice...

Seasonal Adjustment

The Three Snowmen

The Two Wisemen

Myrrh Bust

Rowdy Guests

Rough Christmas

Silent Knight

God Bless Everyone!

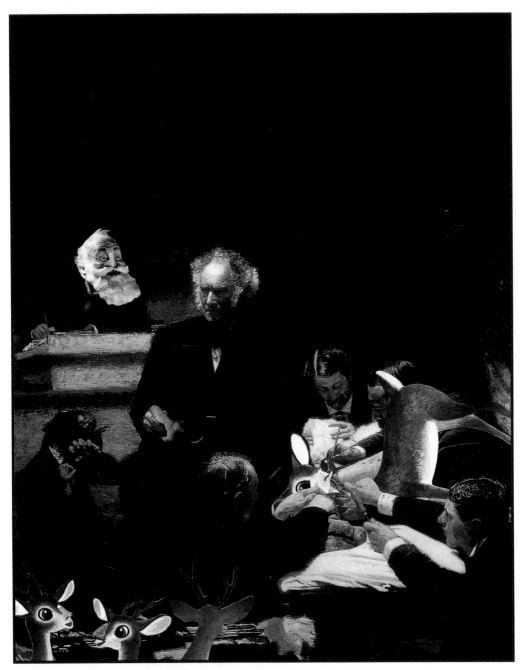

Rhinoplastic Christmas

One for the Road

Home Early

Sometimes you just have to make a choice. Sometimes they can pick you, but you just refuse. They can subvert what is beautiful and holy and make it into a circus of gaudy mythological caricatures. Sometimes you just forget you're a virgin.

Maintaining Traditional Values

Downsizing

Repo Claus

That Won't Be Necessary

Holiday Suspect

Holiday Mob

Serial Snowman

Right to Remain Silent Night

Don't Ask, Don't Tell

The Santa Bar

44

The Grateful Sailor

wild party at
Vance's place. Looks like somebody
had just a little too much fun.
Hope the paramedics can revive him
in time for his big evening.
Elves just want to have fun, too
I don't know who that guy in the
front...

Christmas at Arles

Madonna of the Happy Hour

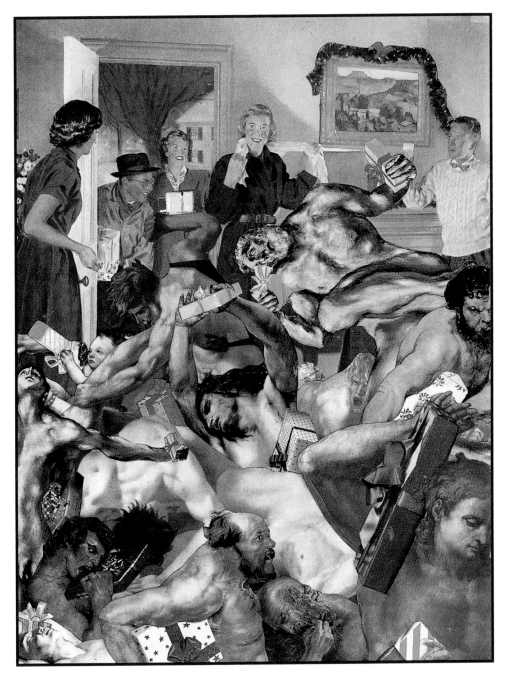

Exchanging Gifts

Samurai Christmas

He Knows When You Are Sleeping

Good News, Bad News

Elf-arazzi

Elf-Preservation

Kicking Back

...Pretty much a dead
(pardon me) heat between this image
and "Damn!" for my best-selling
Christmas card. Another one they
said wouldn't make it breaching
Christmas?!

That never stopped Rembrandt (The
Anatomy Lesson of Dr. [Tulp]), who I
finally got to take out of his
typical dark venue and graft into a
more pleasant environment. Put them
in a greenhouse from a 1950
catalog. [...] pull out some cookies
and candy, and by gosh, that bunch
[doctor wouldn't] go gloomy [...]
But one looks like one of them
lost control. He just had [to] eat
the fruitcake.

THE fruitcake.

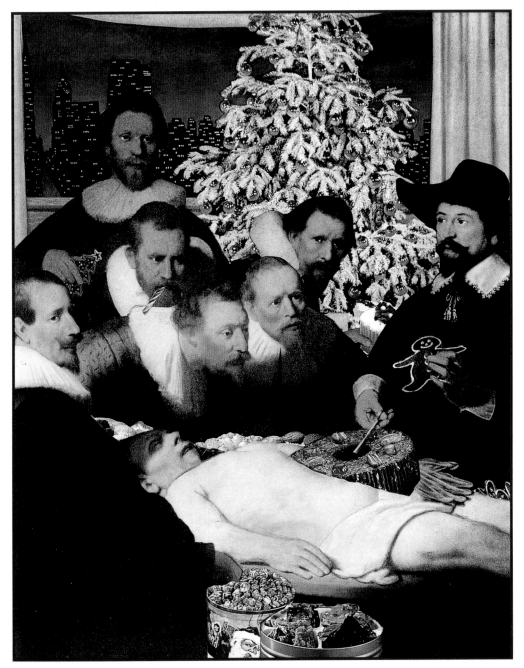

Cause of Death

The Canadians Are Baffled

THE LIST OF PLATES

Canadians are Baffled, The   *62*

Cause of Death   *61*

Christmas at Arles   *47*

Damn!   *9*

Don't Ask, Don't Tell   *43*

Downsizing   *34*

Elf-arazzi   *56*

Elf-Preservation   *57*

Exchanging Gifts   *49*

Expedition   *15*

God Bless Everyone!   *27*

Good News, Bad News   *55*

Grateful Sailor, The   *45*

Hazards Incumbent in the
  Adaptation of Traditional Myth
  to a Redefined Urban Ecosystem   *10*

He Began to Dance Around   *41*

He Knows When You Are Sleeping   *53*

Holiday Mob   *39*

Holiday Suspect   *37*

Home Early   *31*

Kicking Back   *59*

Madonna of the Happy Hour   *48*

Maintaining Traditional Values   *33*

Meat Tonight!   *17*

Myrrh Bust   *22*

North Pole Man   *13*

One for the Road   *30*

Oy!   *51*

Poachers   *16*

Repo Claus   *35*

Rhinoplastic Christmas   *29*

Right to Remain Silent Night   *42*

Rough Christmas   *25*

Rowdy Guests   *23*

Samurai Christmas   *50*

Santa Bar, The   *44*

Seasonal Adjustment   *19*

Serial Snowman   *40*

Silent Knight   *26*

That Won't Be Necessary   *36*

Three Snowmen, The   *20*

Turbulence   *11*

Two Wisemen, The   *21*

ABOUT THE ARTIST

*B*arry Kite received his B.F.A. in film from UCLA. He spent several years writing and performing his own surreal style of poetry before deciding to devote himself to the art of collage. His works have won several art competition awards and can be found in many private as well as corporate collections. His first book, *Sunday Afternoon, Looking for the Car: The Aberrant Art of Barry Kite* (Pomegranate), was published in 1997, and his collages have been featured in several calendars, a book of postcards, as notecards, and, of course, as Christmas cards. Kite lives in northern California, where he also participates in local theater.